To My Beautiful Daughter

ISBN: 978-1-59842-829-2

◖ and Blue Mountain Press are registered in U.S. Patent and Trademark Office. Certain trademarks are used under license.

Printed in China.
Third Printing: 2015

⊕ This book is printed on recycled paper.

This book is printed on paper that has been specially produced to be acid free (neutral pH) and contains no groundwood or unbleached pulp. It conforms with the requirements of the American National Standards Institute, Inc., so as to ensure that this book will last and be enjoyed by future generations.

Blue Mountain Arts, Inc.
P.O. Box 4549, Boulder, Colorado 80306

To My Beautiful Daughter

JENNY KEMPE

Blue Mountain Press™
Boulder, Colorado

From the beginning…
you were perfect.

You are grace.
You are beauty.

My world lights up
with your laughter.

You are my constant pride…

...and my constant worry.

You have a heart of gold...

...that gets easily attached.

You know how to make friends…

...and how to keep them.

You have always had an eye
for beautiful things.

You are clever and strong.
Whatever you put
your mind to,
you can do.

Although we don't always
see things the same way…

...know that deep down,
I accept and love
everything you are.

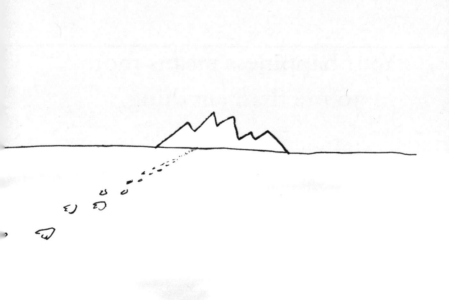

Your happiness means more
to me than anything.

Your joy is my joy.

Your pain is my pain.

You are your own person.

I have accepted that
you make your own decisions
and you have a style
all your own.

I have!

You have found
your own adventures and skills
and ambitions to fulfill.

You've got places to be
and friends to see;
hips to shake and hearts to break;
sales to find and shoes to buy;
sights to see and a world to save.

There's no mountain
too high for you…

Wherever you want to go,
whatever you want to do:
I know you will find your way.

Beautiful daughter,
you have always been my joy,
my most precious treasure.

I am immensely proud of you.

I love you more
than words can say.

2016

Yer Mom

About the Author

In 2009, overwhelmed by the endless bad news in the media, Jenny Kempe decided to take a six-month break from newspapers, TV, and radio. She turned her focus to the things in life that made her happy: friends, family, and taking time to just be. As a result, Jenny created this wonderfully bright and positive gift book that is designed to put a smile on the face of someone you care for.